MW00882699

## Westward Expansion
### AMERICA'S PUSH TO THE PACIFIC

# NATIVE AMERICAN TREATMENT AND RESISTANCE

### PHILIP WOLNY

Britannica
Educational Publishing

IN ASSOCIATION WITH

ROSEN
EDUCATIONAL SERVICES

Published in 2018 by Britannica Educational Publishing (a trademark of Encyclopædia Britannica, Inc.) in association with The Rosen Publishing Group, Inc. 29 East 21st Street, New York, NY 10010

Distributed exclusively by Rosen Publishing.
To see additional Britannica Educational Publishing titles, go to rosenpublishing.com.

First Edition

**Britannica Educational Publishing**
J.E. Luebering: Executive Director, Core Editorial
Andrea R. Field: Managing Editor, Compton's by Britannica

**Rosen Publishing**
Heather Moore Niver: Editor
Nelson Sá: Art Director
Tahara Anderson: Series Designer
Cindy Reiman: Photography Manager
Heather Moore Niver: Photo Researcher

**Library of Congress Cataloging-in-Publication Data**

Names: Wolny, Philip, author.
Title: Native American treatment and resistance / Philip Wolny.
Description: New York : Britannica Educational Publishing, in Association with Rosen Educational Services, 2018 | Series: Westward expansion: America's push to the Pacific | Includes bibliographical references and index. | Audience: Grades 5–8.
Identifiers: LCCN 2017018666| ISBN 9781680487954 (library bound) | ISBN 9781680487947 (pbk.) | ISBN 9781538300152 (6 pack)
Subjects: LCSH: Indians, Treatment of—North America—Juvenile literature. | Indians of North America—Government relations—Juvenile literature. | Indians of North America—Wars—Juvenile literature. | United States—Territorial expansion—Juvenile literature.
Classification: LCC E93 .W84 2018 | DDC 970.004/97—dc23
LC record available at https://lccn.loc.gov/2017018666

*Manufactured in the United States of America*

**Photo credits:** Cover, cover and interior pages (banner) Library of Congress Prints and Photographs Division; p. 5 Pacific Press/LightRocket/Getty Images; p. 9 Fotosearch/Archive Photos/Getty Images; p. 10 Lives of Famous Indian Chiefs by Norman B. Wood., 1906; p. 12 Bettmann/Getty Images; p. 13 Emmet Collection, New York Public Library Digital Collection (420573); p. 15 Library of Congress, Washington, D.C.; p. 18 Library of Congress, Washington, D.C. (LC-USZ62-110274); p. 19 © A Historical Narrative of the Civil and Military Services of Major-General William H. Harrison by Moses Dawson, 1824; pp. 22, 34 Encyclopædia Britannica, Inc.; p. 23 Al Moldvay/Denver Post/Getty Images; pp. 24, 35, 38 MPI/Archive Photos/Getty Images; p. 27 Library of Congress, Washington, D.C. (digital id: ppmsca 09855); p. 28 Historical/Corbis Historical/Getty Images; p. 29 Library of Congress, Washington, D.C. (neg. no. LC-USZ62-36613); p. 30 Universal Images Group/Getty Images; p. 32 Danita Delimont/Alamy Stock Photo; p. 36 Library of Congress, Washington, D.C. (neg. no. LC-USZ62-91032); p. 41 Ralph Crane/The LIFE Picture Collection/Getty Images.

# CONTENTS

# INTRODUCTION

In 2016, a new dispute arose over a piece of land with a long history of conflict. The controversial project known as the Dakota Access Pipeline was the center of a high-profile protest in North Dakota by the Sioux Indians of the Standing Rock Reservation and their allies. The route of the oil pipeline was to run under a reservoir that serves as the main water source for the reservation.

The Standing Rock Sioux feared that the project would pollute their water supply and damage sites that were sacred to them. Over the course of several months, the Sioux and thousands of supporters gathered at the site to make their voices heard. The tribe also resisted in the courts, filing a lawsuit against the US Army Corps of Engineers, which had approved the pipeline.

The protests received international attention. Millions watching worldwide admired the courage of those who called themselves "water protectors."

A months-long demonstration against the Dakota Access Pipeline in North Dakota was led by "water protectors" from the Standing Rock Sioux Reservation.

Violent crackdowns by police and other security officers included the use of water cannons, rubber bullets, and other heavy-handed methods. Such tactics made many people sympathize with the protesters.

The Standing Rock Sioux won a victory in late 2016 when the administration of President Barack Obama halted construction of the pipeline until an environmental review of the route was completed. But after Donald Trump took the presidency in 2017, construction was allowed to resume.

The pipeline fight was only the latest in a long string of conflicts between Native American peoples and those who have sought to control their land or deny their rights. There is much to admire about the expansion of the United States from the colonial era to its status as a world power. But the displacement and destruction of Native American cultures during this period represented the dark side of "progress."

In the early years of the American colonies, Native Americans and the newly arrived settlers sometimes lived peacefully side by side. The harvest feast shared by the Wampanoag Indians and the Pilgrims in Massachusetts in 1621—commemorated in the annual Thanksgiving holiday—is the most famous example of friendly relations in the colonies. Even before that event, however, disputes between Native Americans and colonists had erupted into conflict elsewhere in New England. Warfare would become increasingly common as the colonies, and then the United States, pushed farther westward. Eventually the US government would make hundreds of treaties that were supposed to guarantee the rights of Indian peoples. In the end, however, these treaties proved to be little more than a long series of broken promises.

For many generations, the cycle of mistreatment by the United States and resistance by Native Americans would be a recurring theme as the country expanded westward. The lengthy and brutal conflict between Indians and whites is one of the most tragic chapters in US history. Yet while the military conquest of the Indians was completed long ago, the spirit of resistance among Native Americans remains strong to this day.

# CHAPTER ONE

# WHOSE LAND?

Although native peoples had lived in North and South America for thousands of years, the continents were unknown to Europeans when Christopher Columbus landed in the Caribbean islands in 1492. Sailing for Spain, he had been searching for a sea route from Europe to Asia. Columbus did not find a new trade route, but his voyage paved the way for European exploration of what became known as the New World.

European powers competed with one another to find riches or to plant colonies in the new lands. Spain conquered the Aztec and Inca empires in Mexico and South America before turning northward to claim large parts of what would become the southern and south-western United States. France claimed territories in what are now the eastern United States and Canada. It was England, however, that established the colonies that would become the United States.

A Native American army battles Spanish explorer Hernando de Soto and his soldiers in the village of Mabila in what is now central Alabama in about 1540.

The population of Native Americans in what is now the continental United States before the arrival of Europeans is unknown, but it has been estimated in the millions. The subsequent history of the American colonies and then the United States cannot be discussed without considering the role of the Indians. As a whole, the Indians were an important influence on the Europeans who settled in the New World. Nevertheless, relations between the groups were characterized mainly by tension and conflict.

## AN OLD WORLD GREETS A NEW ONE

Beginning with Jamestown in 1607, the English set up colonies along the Atlantic coast of North America. At first the local Native Americans helped the English colonists establish settlements, raise crops, and adjust to living in an environment that was quite different from England's. Powhatan (Wahunsenacah), leader of an Algonquian-speaking confederacy in Virginia, and

Powhatan was the leader of the Powhatan confederacy of American Indians. This image is taken from Norman B. Wood's 1906 book *The Lives of Famous Indian Chiefs.*

Massasoit (Wasamegin), leader of the Wampanoag Indians in New England, established generally peaceful trade relations with the English. But the spirit of friendship deteriorated as the expanding colonies pressed further into Indian territory, routinely breaking their boundary agreements.

A difference of attitudes over land ownership was a major cause of conflict between

Indians and Europeans. Few Native American peoples had developed a system of private land ownership as Europeans understood it. Instead, within the boundaries of each tribe's territory, all members of the tribe used the land communally. No individual owned any of the land, and no one person, not even a tribal leader, could sell it. While European settlers thought they were obtaining permanent title to Indian lands by purchase, the Indian peoples saw it as an agreement only to share or rent the land.

## EARLY CONFLICTS

By 1609, the Jamestown region of Virginia was experiencing a third year of severe drought. In response to English thievery (mostly of food), Powhatan prohibited the trading of food to the colonists. He also began to attack any colonists who left the Jamestown fort. These actions contributed to a period of starvation for the colony (1609–1611) that nearly caused its abandonment.

After Powhatan's death in 1618, his brother and successor, Opechancanough, tried to force the colonists out. In 1622, his men launched attacks against Jamestown that killed some 350 of the 1,200 colonists. The so-called Powhatan War continued off and on until 1644, eventually resulting in a new boundary

In a short but vicious war, English colonists destroyed the main Pequot village in Connecticut in 1637. Some six hundred Pequot were burned alive or slaughtered.

agreement between the Indians and the colonists. The fighting ended only after a series of epidemics had devastated the region's Indian population, which shrank as the English population grew. Within five years, colonists were once again trespassing in Powhatan territory.

Another early clash between Indians and whites took place in Connecticut. During the Pequot War of 1636–1637, colonists attacked the main village of the Pequot people. About six hundred Indians were killed, and the Pequot tribe was virtually destroyed.

# METACOM AND KING PHILIP'S WAR

Also called Metacomet, Metacom was the second son of Massasoit—a grand sachem, or chief, of the Wampanoag who oversaw a lifetime of peaceful relations with the Pilgrims and other New England settlers. Massasoit died in 1661, and Metacom's older brother, Alexander, assumed the role of chief. Upon Alexander's death the following year, Metacom became sachem of the Wampanoag.

For some time, Indians of New England had been exchanging land for British guns, ammunition, liquor, and blankets. Metacom assembled an alliance of Indian peoples to oppose the settlers. The conflict known as King Philip's

War erupted in 1675 when colonial authorities executed three Wampanoag for murder. A year later, with the Indians near defeat, Metacom was betrayed by a Wampanoag informer and killed in a final battle. Metacom was beheaded and quartered, and his head was displayed on a pole in the Plymouth Colony for twenty-five years.

Metacom

In 1675, various Indian tribes in New England formed an alliance to resist white settlement. It was led by Massasoit's son Metacom, who was called King Philip by the colonists. Metacom's forces were at first victorious, but after a year of savage fighting they were defeated. Some six hundred Europeans and three thousand Indians had been killed.

## COLONIAL RIVALRIES AND NATIVE ALLIANCES

By the end of the 1600s, the land struggles of Native Americans became caught up in a series of wars between England and France for dominance in North America. Some Indians aided the English, while others helped the French. Ultimately the English prevailed. Under the peace treaty that ended the French and Indian War in 1763, France turned over to England its colonies east of the Mississippi River. England now ruled a vast territory reaching from Hudson Bay to the Gulf of Mexico and from the Atlantic coast to the Mississippi River.

With English rule came a new flood of settlers. Like earlier emigrants, they often trespassed on native lands. Some Indians took advantage of the disorder near the end of the French and Indian War to attack the settlers. In 1763, the Ottawa leader Pontiac led a coalition of tribes in capturing several English forts near the Great

In this lithograph from James Wimer's *Events in Indian History* (1841), the Ottawa leader Pontiac meets with Major Robert Rogers, a colonial militia leader, in 1760.

Lakes. In response to Pontiac's War, the English issued the Proclamation of 1763, one of the most important documents in Native American legal history. The proclamation declared as Indian territory the land between the Appalachian Mountains and the Mississippi River and from the Great Lakes almost to the Gulf of Mexico. It forbade European settlement on this territory and ordered those settlers already there to leave. Nevertheless, thousands of settlers ignored the orders and moved into the reserved territory.

# A NEW NATION IS BORN

Disputes between the settlers and the British government eventually led to the American Revolution of
1775–1783. In this war the English colonies won their
independence. Many Indian tribes fought for the British
government, who posed as defenders of Indian land
against the colonists. Indian aid provoked retaliatory
campaigns by the colonial army, including one led by
General John Sullivan on the Iroquois people of New
York. The British defeat and the rise of a new American
nation left many Native Americans wondering about
their role in the new era.

# CHAPTER TWO

# THE OPENING OF THE WEST

After the American Revolution, the new US government hoped to maintain peace with the Native Americans on the frontier. The government promised that the Proclamation of 1763 would be honored. The first full declaration of US policy toward the Indians was embodied in the Northwest Ordinance of 1787:

*The utmost good faith shall always be observed toward the Indians, their lands and property shall never be taken from them without their consent; and in their property, rights, and liberty, they shall never be invaded or disturbed, unless in just and lawful wars authorized by Congress; but laws founded in justice and humanity shall from time to time be made, for preventing wrongs being done to them, and for preserving peace and friendship with them.*

The US government sought to manage its relations with American Indian tribes through treaties. Beginning in 1778, the government negotiated hundreds of treaties in which tribes agreed to give up much of their territory. In exchange, the Indians typically received goods, money, and promises that US citizens would not settle on the tribes' remaining lands. Nevertheless, as the United States continued to expand westward, settlers built and farmed on lands that had been reserved for the Indians. The result was decades of conflict between Indians and the US government.

WAYNE'S DEFEAT OF THE INDIANS.

US General Anthony Wayne's victory over the Northwest Indian Confederation in the Battle of Fallen Timbers ended two decades of border warfare in the Ohio Valley.

## BATTLE FOR THE OHIO VALLEY

Some of the earliest battles took place in the Ohio River valley. When the Indians raided American settlements on their lands, the US government responded with force. The Indians, in turn, formed an alliance called the Northwest Indian Confederation, consisting mainly of Shawnee, Delaware, Ottawa, Iroquois, Ojibwa, Miami, and Potawatomi. The Indians defeated US troops in 1790 and 1791 but were crushed in the Battle of Fallen Timbers in 1794. In 1795, the Miami chief Little Turtle, representing the confederation, signed the Treaty of Fort Greenville, ceding to the United States most of Ohio and parts of Indiana, Illinois, and Michigan.

The treaty accelerated westward migration and settlement of the Ohio Valley. In 1809, William Henry Harrison, a US military leader and governor of the Indiana Territory, signed the Treaty of Fort Wayne with a number of Indian tribes, including the Miami, Delaware, Potawatomi, and Kickapoo. The agreement ceded to the United States more than three million acres (1,214,000

General William Henry Harrison led the US troops that defeated the British and their Indian allies under Tecumseh at the Battle of the Thames in Ontario, Canada, in 1813.

hectares) of Indian land in what are now Indiana and Illinois.

Tecumseh, a Shawnee leader, strongly opposed the treaty. He organized several tribes to resist further ceding of Indian lands. A group of Shawnee led by Tecumseh's brother Tenskwatawa was defeated in 1811 by General Harrison at the Battle of Tippecanoe. During the War of 1812, Tecumseh's coalition sided with the British and won a number of early victories. In the end, however, they were defeated.

# INDIAN REMOVAL

After the War of 1812, US government policy focused

## TECUMSEH

The Shawnee chief Tecumseh led Native American resistance to white rule in the Ohio River valley. Born in what is now Ohio in 1768, he grew up witnessing suffering brought to his people by white settlers. In 1808, Tecumseh and his brother Tenskwatawa, a religious leader known as "The Prophet," founded a village called Prophetstown in northern Indiana. They persuaded the Indians who lived there to avoid liquor, tend their land, and reject white culture in favor of native traditions.

Meanwhile, Tecumseh formed a defensive confederacy of Indian peoples. He made long journeys throughout the East and Midwest to recruit allies. He reportedly told them, "Our fathers, from their tombs, reproach us as slaves and cowards."

Tecumseh demanded that Indiana governor (and future US president) William Henry Harrison return lands that tribes had given up in what is now Indiana and Illinois. Since the land belonged to all of the Indians, Tecumseh argued, individual chiefs did not have the right to give it away. His demand was rejected. He then traveled to Canada to consult the British and afterward to the Southwest to enlist support of Indian peoples there. While Tecumseh was away, Harrison's troops defeated a Shawnee force led by Tenskwatawa in the Battle of Tippecanoe.

When the War of 1812 broke out between the United States and Britain, Tecumseh joined his forces with British troops just over the Canadian border. The combined force captured Detroit, along with 2,500 US soldiers. In October 1813, Tecumseh was killed while fighting Harrison's troops in what is now southern Ontario. His death marked the end of Indian resistance in the Ohio River valley and most of the lower Midwest and South.

on the removal of Native Americans to areas west of the Mississippi River—to the so-called Great American Desert (the Great Plains), where, supposedly, no white man would ever want to live. To implement this policy, President Andrew Jackson

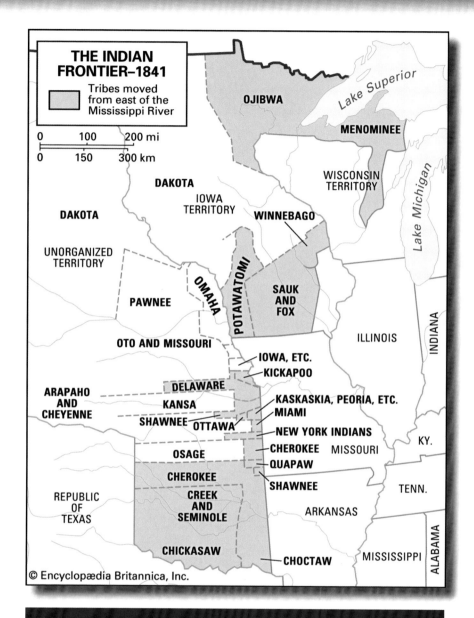

## THE INDIAN FRONTIER–1841

Tribes moved from east of the Mississippi River

0    100    200 mi
0    150    300 km

OJIBWA

Lake Superior

MENOMINEE

WISCONSIN TERRITORY

Lake Michigan

DAKOTA

IOWA TERRITORY

WINNEBAGO

DAKOTA

UNORGANIZED TERRITORY

OMAHA

POTAWATOMI

SAUK AND FOX

PAWNEE

OTO AND MISSOURI

ILLINOIS

INDIANA

IOWA, ETC.

KICKAPOO

DELAWARE

ARAPAHO AND CHEYENNE

KANSA

KASKASKIA, PEORIA, ETC.

MIAMI

SHAWNEE OTTAWA

NEW YORK INDIANS

KY.

CHEROKEE    MISSOURI

OSAGE

QUAPAW

CHEROKEE

SHAWNEE

TENN.

REPUBLIC OF TEXAS

CREEK AND SEMINOLE

ARKANSAS

CHICKASAW

ALABAMA

CHOCTAW    MISSISSIPPI

© Encyclopædia Britannica, Inc.

Under pressure from settlers who wanted new farmland, the United States government relocated tens of thousands of Eastern Indians to the Great Plains during the 1830s and 1840s.

signed the Indian Removal Act into law on May 28, 1830. The president was a dedicated foe of the Indians, having led campaigns against the Creek and Seminole peoples during his earlier military career. The Indian Removal Act gave Jackson the power to grant Indian tribes land west of the Mississippi in exchange for their land east of the river.

A number of northern tribes were peacefully resettled in western lands. The problem lay in the Southeast, where some members of what were known as the Five Civilized Tribes refused to accept the order. Within a few years, three of these tribes—the Choctaw, Creek, and Chickasaw—agreed to head west to the newly created Indian Territory (now Oklahoma). But the other two—the Cherokee and the Seminole—kept up their resistance.

## THE TRAIL OF TEARS

The Cherokee used legal action to oppose removal. In 1832, the US Supreme Court ruled that the Cherokee could

Blackbear Bosin, a painter and sculptor of Comanche-Kiowa origin, made this 1951 painting evoking the sadness and defeat of the Trail of Tears.

retain their lands in Georgia. Georgia did not follow the Court's decision, however, and Jackson refused to enforce it.

In 1838, the US military began to force Cherokee people from their homes, often at gunpoint. Held in miserable prison camps for days or weeks before their journeys began, many Cherokee became ill, and most were poorly prepared for the very difficult trip. With inadequate food, shelter, and clothing, the Cherokee suffered terribly on the march, especially after cold weather arrived. About 4,000 of the estimated 15,000 Cherokee died on the 116-day journey, many because the escorting troops refused to slow or stop so that the ill and exhausted could recover. This bitter trek has become known as the Trail of Tears.

The Seminole leader Osceola confounded the United States while leading a resistance movement in Florida before his 1837 capture.

## SEMINOLE WARS

The Seminole fiercely resisted removal. This

Florida tribe had already been involved in one conflict with the US government. In 1817, US troops led by then-General Andrew Jackson invaded Seminole territory to recapture runaway slaves who had found safe haven among the tribe. The US troops burned Seminole towns in the conflict, which became known as the First Seminole War.

Following this war, the Seminole were forced to move to a reservation in central Florida. But the Indian Removal Act required them to give up this land, too. Seminole resistance to the act sparked the Second Seminole War in 1835. Seminole warriors, led by the dynamic chief Osceola, hid their families in the Everglades and fought to defend their homeland using guerrilla tactics.

In October 1837, Osceola and several other Seminole leaders went to St. Augustine, Florida, hoping to negotiate a truce. They were instead seized and imprisoned. Only after Osceola's capture did Indian resistance decline. After the war ended in 1842, most of the remaining Seminole agreed to emigrate. As many as two thousand US soldiers had been killed in this deadliest and costliest of all wars fought between the United States and Indian tribes.

# CHAPTER THREE

# "FROM SEA TO SHINING SEA"

By the end of the 1840s, except for small segments of tribes who had fled to remote areas, most Native Americans of the Northeast and Southeast had been forced out of their original territories. American settlers, however, were hungry for even more land. They believed in Manifest Destiny—the idea that the United States had a divinely assigned mission to expand westward and spread democratic and Protestant ideals across North America. The goal was a nation that stretched from the Atlantic Ocean to the Pacific—"from sea to shining sea." During the westward push, Native Americans were seen merely as an obstacle to be overcome.

## THE NORTHWEST

Numerous clashes erupted in the Pacific Northwest when thousands of white settlers poured into the

A woman leading pioneers and railroads westward—representing the concept of Manifest Destiny—is the central figure in this color print of John Gast's 1872 painting titled *American Progress*.

Oregon Territory after its acquisition from Great Britain in 1846. In the 1850s, wars broke out around Puget Sound after some tribes were deceived into signing treaties giving away much of their land. The Indians were quickly defeated, however, and confined to reservations.

In other areas of the Northwest, war continued into the late 1870s. In 1877, the Nez Percé people, led by Chief Joseph (Hinmaton-yalatkit), were

Even after surrendering to the United States, Nez Percé leader Chief Joseph continued to speak out against the mistreatment of American Indians until his death in 1904.

defeated after refusing to agree to treaties ceding nearly all their land to the United States. Hardships resulting from loss of land, lack of food, and disease led to an unsuccessful uprising of the Bannock Indians of Idaho in 1878.

## THE SOUTHWEST

The Southwest came under US control as a result of the Mexican-American War of 1846–1848. In 1847, Pueblo Indians rose up against settlers at Taos (later in New Mexico) and were defeated. But relations between settlers and the Pueblo, Pima, and Tohono O'odham (Papago) were usually peaceful.

The Navajo and Apache retaliated when settlers seized their lands and destroyed their animals and gardens. The Navajo were overpowered in the 1860s and forced onto a reservation, but the Apache fought on. Even after they too were restricted to reservations, small bands continued to mount raids. When the Apache leader Geronimo (Goyathlay) finally surrendered in 1886, Indians in the Southwest ended their military resistance to colonization.

Geronimo led the Chiricahua Apache in attacks on the Mexican and US militaries. In 1886, outmatched by thousands of US troops, he was finally forced to surrender.

# CALIFORNIA

The Mexican-American War also gave the United States control of California. The discovery of gold in 1848 brought tens of thousands of prospectors to California, which entered the Union in 1850. Miners drove Native Americans off their traditional lands, depriving them

GOLD MINING IN CALIFORNIA.

This Currier and Ives lithograph depicts a scene from the California Gold Rush of the 1840s and 1850s, which brought fortune seekers into conflict with the Native Americans of the soon-to-be state.

of their usual food sources. Indians fought back by raiding mining settlements and other communities. This brought brutal reprisals, and thousands of Indians were killed. Others were enslaved, including children who had been kidnapped.

Many of California's surviving Indians were moved to reservations, where living conditions were poor and starvation was common. By 1870, the

## THE BUREAU OF INDIAN AFFAIRS

The first federal agency charged with overseeing how the United States government dealt with Indian treaties was placed under the secretary of war by Congress in 1789. The Bureau of Indian Affairs (BIA) was created within the War Department in 1824 and was transferred to the new Department of the Interior in 1849.

The BIA was supposed to enforce the restrictions against whites on Indian lands and to help Indians sell or lease their land when it was legal to do so. The agency was also supposed to manage the money deposited in the US Treasury to the credit of Indian tribes in payment for land. Unfortunately, the BIA was notoriously corrupt. As a result, many Indian lands were illegally sold or even stolen.

number of Indians in California, believed to be as large as 150,000 before the Gold Rush, had declined to about 30,000.

## THE PLAINS

In about 1850, Native Americans of the Great Plains began attacking wagon trains carrying settlers

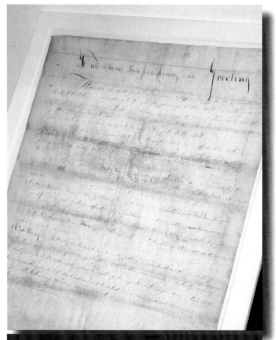

The Fort Laramie Treaty of 1851 is displayed at the Three Affiliated Tribes Museum on the Fort Berthold Indian Reservation in North Dakota.

westward. They were angered by ill treatment from the settlers and by the driving away of bison herds on which they were dependent for food, clothing, and shelter. Efforts by the US Army and the government to preserve peace led to the Fort Laramie Treaty of 1851. The Plains tribes promised to confine themselves to designated hunting grounds, and the government agreed to keep settlers out of those areas. This treaty would prove to be as ineffective as so many that had come before.

# CHAPTER FOUR

# LAST STAND AND LEGACY

Over the next few decades, the expansion of American settlements on the Great Plains led to some of the most intense battles between Native Americans and the United States. In these conflicts, known as the Plains Wars, a number of tribes offered stiff resistance. By the end of the 1800s, however, the military conquest of the American Indians would be complete. After that, Indian peoples had to find new forms of resistance for the twentieth and twenty-first centuries.

## THE SIOUX NATION TAKES A STAND

Some of the latest and fiercest resistance put up by Native Americans came from the tribes that made up the Great Sioux Nation in the northern Great Plains.

**INDIAN WARS ON THE PLAINS**

- ⚔ Major battle or incident
- —— Modern international boundaries
- - - - Modern state/province boundaries

CANADA

⚔ Bear Paw Mountain (1877)

BLACKFEET

HIDATSA

CROW

MANDAN

⚔ Little Bighorn (1876)

SIOUX

ARIKARA

SIOUX

⚔ Fetterman Massacre (1866)

CHEYENNE

SIOUX   ⚔ New Ulm (1862)

⚔ Wounded Knee (1890)

OMAHA

IOWA

PAWNEE

OTO

ARAPAHO

MISSOURI

KANSA

UNITED STATES

⚔ Sand Creek Massacre (1864)

KIOWA

OSAGE

⚔ Washita River (1868)

⚔ Red River War (1874–75)

WICHITA

COMANCHE

MEXICO

© Encyclopædia Britannica, Inc.

In the second half of the 1800s, American Indians and US forces fought a number of battles for control of the Great Plains. Some events of this period, however, are more accurately called massacres.

The Sioux were not a single tribe, but rather an alliance of tribes who spoke related languages.

After the Fort Laramie Treaty was signed in 1851, the Sioux group known as the Santee (or Dakota) gave up most of their land in what is now Minnesota. They agreed to move to a reservation in return for promises of food and cash from the US government. When these promises were broken, the Dakota rebelled. Led by Little Crow, the Dakota killed four hundred settlers and seventy US soldiers in what

WHITNEY, **LITTLE CROW,** ST. PAUL.
C Sionx Chief. and Leader of the *Indian Massacre of 1862*, in Minnesota

.tered according to Act in Congress, by J. E. Whitney, in the year 1862
in the Clerk's Office of the U. S. Court for Minnesota.

Chief Little Crow was a Santee Sioux leader who led a major uprising against settlers in Minnesota. The caption identifies him as "leader of the Indian Massacre of 1862."

became known as the Sioux Uprising of 1862. As punishment, thirty-eight Santee were hanged in the largest mass execution in US history.

In 1865, the US government violated earlier treaties by starting construction of forts and a wagon road

In the 1860s, Red Cloud led the Oglala Sioux in campaigns that prevented the US Army from opening the Bozeman Trail to the Montana goldfields.

to mining camps in the Montana Territory. In response, the Oglala Sioux under Red Cloud (Mahpiua Luta) attacked and destroyed several forts. Under a new peace treaty of 1868, the government stopped the road construction, dismantled the forts, and again guaranteed the Indian reserve. But it was only a brief delay of the tragedy to come.

In 1871, the US Congress declared that Indian tribes were no longer to be recognized as sovereign powers with whom treaties must be made. Although existing treaties were supposedly still valid, they were constantly violated. The treaty of 1868 had made the Black Hills of the Dakota Territory part of a large Sioux reservation. But the discovery of gold there in 1874 brought a stampede of gold seekers.

# LITTLE BIGHORN AND WOUNDED KNEE

In 1875, the Sioux refused to sell the Black Hills land to the government, which then ordered them out of the area and onto other reservations. When the Sioux refused, US Army troops led by Lieutenant Colonel George A. Custer were sent to evict them. On June 25, 1876, the government troops attacked a large group of Sioux, Northern Cheyenne, and Arapaho. The fight that followed is known as the Battle of the Little Bighorn, after the river where it took place. The main body of Indians, under the Sioux leaders Sitting Bull (Tatanka Iyotake) and Crazy Horse (Tashunke Witko), wiped out Custer and his two hundred men. It was one of the most famous US military defeats of all time—memorialized as "Custer's Last Stand."

It was also the last major military victory of any Indian force. Gradually, most Indians were rounded up and confined to reservations. During this time a new spiritual movement arose among tribes of the Plains. Known as the Ghost Dance, the cult predicted that the white man would be wiped out and the natural, old order restored if enough Indians would perform certain dances and songs.

Sitting Bull was killed by Indian police as they tried to suppress the Ghost Dance at Standing Rock Reservation in North Dakota. In 2016–2017 the reservation was the site of protests against the Dakota Access Pipeline.

The Ghost Dance movement was crushed in 1890. Sitting Bull was killed as authorities tried to arrest him. Two weeks later, on December 29, 1890, the US Army killed more than two hundred Indian men, women, and children at the village of Wounded Knee in South Dakota. Almost four hundred years after the arrival of Columbus, the massacre at Wounded Knee completed the military conquest of the American Indian. Across the continent, however, most groups continued to resist in other ways, such as by maintaining their traditional languages and religious practices.

# ALLOTMENT AND ASSIMILATION

By the late 1800s, most Indians were restricted to reservations. Many whites, regarding ownership of land as the basis of success, hoped that by owning their own farms the Indians would become independent farmers. Other whites, hungry for land, thought that too much land had already been reserved for the Indians. In addition, many whites thought that the government support of Indians was a kind of charity rather than a legal obligation.

All of these groups of whites urged the passage of the Dawes General Allotment Act of 1887. This act provided for dividing reservations, which had been held in common by the tribes, into parcels to be allotted to individual Indians. The so-called "surplus" land was eventually sold to white settlers. The act resulted in the loss of tens of millions of acres of Indian land. Many Indians were unused to the idea of individual ownership of land and had little understanding of money. They sold their allotments at very low prices, spent the money, and became poor.

At the same time, the government tried to assimilate, or integrate, Indians into the mainstream culture. One method of assimilation was the boarding, or residential, school. From the mid-1800s until as late as the 1960s, the US government forced many Native American families to send their children to these schools. The instruction was designed to eliminate any use of traditional language, behavior, or

*(Continued on the next page)*

*(Continued from the previous page)*

religion. Arriving children had to trade their traditional clothing for uniforms. Students were often abused physically and verbally in these poorly regulated places.

Assimilation policies were also enforced on reservations. For example, government authorities banned traditional religious practices and dances. Many Indians continued to engage in these practices in secret.

# A LEGACY OF RESISTANCE AND REBIRTH

Given the discrimination Native Americans have faced, it is not surprising that many Indian communities continue to face challenges such as poverty and substance abuse. Native American activists, however, have continued to make progress in their efforts to achieve a better life for their peoples. Key to these efforts has been the pursuit of sovereignty, or self-government. When Native Americans peoples have the authority to make their own decisions concerning the issues that affect them most, they are empowered to shape their communities on their own terms.

Although Native Americans had been fighting for their rights for centuries, their efforts attracted greater notice in the late twentieth century. During the 1960s, as

In November 1969, American Indian activists occupied Alcatraz Island in San Francisco Bay. They refused to leave the island until they were forced off by federal marshals in June 1971.

African Americans campaigned for equality in the civil rights movement, Indians also drew attention to their causes through mass protests. The causes they championed included economic independence, revitalization of traditional culture, and protection of legal rights. Above all was control over tribal areas and the restoration of lands that they believed had been illegally seized.

The American Indian Movement (AIM) took part in many highly publicized protests. For nineteen months in 1969–1971, Indian activists occupied Alcatraz Island in San Francisco Bay (California), claiming it as Indian land.

In 1973, about two hundred armed AIM supporters occupied Wounded Knee, the site of the massacre of 1890. In a seventy-one-day siege, two Indians were killed and one federal marshal was seriously wounded.

In the late twentieth century Native Americans turned increasingly to the courts to press their causes. The rights to forest and mineral resources on tribal lands became the subjects of many lawsuits. Some Native Americans pressed claims to land taken in the nineteenth century and earlier.

# GLOSSARY

**assimilation**  The process of being absorbed into a dominant or mainstream social group.

**confederacy**  An alliance of states, tribes, or other groups united for a common purpose.

**emigrate**  To leave one's nation or home to live elsewhere.

**gold rush**  A rush by many people to newly discovered goldfields.

**Great Plains**  A vast grassland region of North America that reaches from the Rocky Mountains to the Mississippi River and from southern Canada to the US state of Texas.

**guerrilla**  Describes a type of warfare in which fighters attack the enemy in irregular and clever ways.

**Manifest Destiny**  The nineteenth-century idea that the United States had the right and duty to expand from the Atlantic to the Pacific Ocean.

**prospector**  A person who searches for new gold deposits.

**reprisal**  An act of revenge for damage or loss suffered.

**reproach**  To express disapproval or disgust.

**reservation**  A piece of land set aside for the exclusive use of American Indians.

**retaliate**  To repay; to get revenge.

**sovereign**  Self-governing.

# FOR FURTHER READING

Bowes, John P. *Black Hawk and the War of 1832: Removal in the North* (Landmark Events in Native American History). New York, NY: Chelsea House, 2007.

Harasymiw, Mark, and Therese Harasymiw. *Native Americans in Early America* (The Story of America). Milwaukee, WI: Gareth Stevens Publishing, 2011.

Kuiper, Kathleen. *American Indians of California, the Great Basin, and the Southwest.* New York, NY: Britannica Educational Publishing, 2012.

Lawton, Cassie M., and Raymond Bial. *The People and Culture of the Sioux.* New York, NY: Cavendish Square, 2017.

Luebering, J.E., ed. *Native American History* (The Native American Sourcebook). New York, NY: Britannica Educational Publishing, 2011.

Moriarty, J.T. *Manifest Destiny: A Primary Source History of America's Territorial Expansion in the 19th Century.* New York, NY: Rosen Publishing, 2005.

Peppas, Lynn. *Trail of Tears.* New York, NY: Crabtree, 2014.

Zott, Lynn M. *Native Americans* (Opposing Viewpoints). Detroit, MI: Greenhaven Press, 2012.

# WEBSITES

Because of the changing nature of internet links, Rosen Publishing has developed an online list of websites related to the subject of this book. This site is updated regularly. Please use this link to access this list:

http://www.rosenlinks.com/WEST/Resist

# INDEX